MO FARAH

UNAUTHORISED BIOGRAPHY

MICHAEL HURLEY

Raintree is an imprint of Capstone Global Library Limited, a company incorporated in England and Wales having its registered office at 7 Pilgrim Street, London, EC4V 6LB – Registered company number: 6695582

To contact Raintree, please phone
0845 6044371, fax + 44 (0) 1865 312263,
or email myorders@raintreepublishers.co.uk.

Text © Capstone Global Library Limited 2013
First published in 2013
The moral rights of the proprietor have been asserted.

Edited by Charlotte Guillain
Designed by Philippa Jenkins
Picture research by Mica Brancic
Printed and bound in China by CTPS

ISBN 978 1 406 26692 4 (hardback)
17 16 15 14 13
10 9 8 7 6 5 4 3 2 1

ISBN 978 1 406 26694 8 (paperback)
17 16 15 14 13
10 9 8 7 6 5 4 3 2 1

British Library Cataloguing in Publication Data
Hurley, Michael.
Mo Farah. -- (Sport files)
A full catalogue record for this book is available from the British Library.

Acknowledgements
We would like to thank the following for permission to reproduce photographs: © Corbis/AMA/©Catherine Ivill p.**20**; © Getty Images pp.**5** (Michael Steele), **8** (Bob Thomas), **11**, **13** (Bongarts/Alexander Hassenstein), **14** (AFP Photo/Kazuhiro Nogi), **15** (Chris McGrath), **16** (Craig Mitchelldyer), **17** (Sports Illustrated/Lane Stewart), **18** (Harry How), **19** (Mike Hewitt), **21** (Clive Brunskill), **25** (Stu Forster), **26** (Time Life Pictures/Mark Kauffman), **27** (Mark Dadswell), **29** (Oli Scarff); © Getty Images for Aviva p.**9**; © Getty Images for Nike p.**23**; © Newspics Ltd p.**7**; © Press Association/EMPICS Sport/Stephen Pond p.**10**; © Rex Features/Steve Meddle p.**24**.

Cover photograph of Mo Farah reproduced with permission of © Getty Images/Clive Brunskill.

Every effort has been made to contact copyright holders of material reproduced in this book. Any omissions will be rectified in subsequent printings if notice is given to the publisher.

CONTENTS

Some words are printed in bold, **like this**. You can find out what they mean by looking in the glossary.

Mo Farah is a globally successful long-distance athlete. In recent years he has exploded onto the athletics scene and gained the world's attention with his astonishing performances on the track.

This World and Olympic champion has faced struggles and disappointment during his life and career, but Mo has always had the drive and focus to overcome any obstacles. His fierce determination to improve and attain his goals has driven him on to great success. Mo has achieved more than anyone could have imagined when he first set foot on an athletics track as a child. With the support of his family, his teacher, his **coaches**, and his fellow athletes, Mo has transformed from a potential athlete, with a considerable amount of talent, into one of the greatest distance runners in history.

Mo has all the records, medals, and admiration from fans that the very best sportspeople deserve. The greatest stars in any sport have to make **sacrifices** and tough decisions on their way to the top of their chosen sport, and Mo is no exception. He has met every challenge in his life head-on, whether it is moving to a new country, competing in his first race, or going for gold in a major athletics championship. He has proved that difficulties faced in life can always be exceeded by the pride and glory gained from achieving your goals. In Mo's case this is on the track, and when he runs at his best no one can match him.

FAST FACT FILE

Name:	Mohamed Farah
Born:	23 March 1983, Mogadishu, Somalia
Height:	1.65 m (5 ft 5 ins)
Weight:	58 kg (128 lbs)
Favourite sport:	Football
Favourite sportsperson:	Muhammad Ali

Mo Farah celebrates as he crosses the finish line in first place.

Mo Farah was born in Mogadishu, the capital of Somalia, in 1983. Somalia is a country on the east coast of Africa. Mo spent most of his childhood in Djibouti, a country that borders Somalia in the north. Mo lived there with some of his family, including his twin brother, Hassan.

When he was eight years old, Mo moved to London, England, to live with his father, meaning he was suddenly separated from his twin brother and other family members. But after years away from his father, he was thrilled when they were reunited: "Seeing Dad was more exciting than anything else," he has said. It was a tough move for Mo, though, and when he first arrived he didn't speak any English. He also needed to quickly get used to living in a new place that was completely different from everything he knew. He had to adapt to the colder climate and try to fit in and make new friends.

Mo was lucky that the area of London he had moved to was full of people from different countries and cultures. His transition must also have been made easier because he had his father and some of his brothers with him.

TROUBLE IN HIS HOMELAND

When Mo was born, there was already a lot of trouble in Somalia, which meant that he and his family would not stay there for long. A **civil war** was taking place, and the capital Mogadishu was becoming a violent and dangerous place to live. The family soon moved to Djibouti, where life was safer. The decision to send Mo and his older brothers to England and to separate him from his twin and the rest of his family was a very difficult one. Mo's parents wanted him to have the best chance to have a successful life.

Mo competing in a cross-country race as a schoolboy.

Alan Watkinson was a P.E. teacher at Mo's secondary school, Isleworth and Syon School for Boys. Mr Watkinson first noticed Mo's talent for distance running, and he persuaded his pupil to join an athletics club. Mo originally wanted to follow in the footsteps of his footballing heroes, but although he had the energy and the running ability, he didn't quite have the necessary skill to be a footballer.

In October 2012, Mo met up with his former teacher at his old school to present him with the Daily Mirror Teacher of the Year Award. Mo told the pupils assembled, "Alan has been a big part of my life and it's great to see him win this. He told me to join an athletics club and I was like, no! But if it wasn't for him I wouldn't be where I am now. He changed my life." Mr Watkinson always encouraged Mo and even gave up his free time to drive him to the running club after school and on Sunday mornings. It was here that Mo's journey to Olympic success really started.

An inspiration to others

Mo's success on the track and his dedication to his sport make him a **role model** for people to look up to and draw inspiration from. At Mo's former school, a special trophy is awarded each year in his honour. The trophy is named the Mo Farah Cup and it is presented to a pupil who shows remarkable effort, just like Mo.

As a young boy, Mo supported Arsenal football team. He still supports them today!

Mo's inspirational teacher, Alan Watkinson (right),
receives his School Sport Teacher of the Year award.

Mo showed a lot of early promise when he started training to be a distance runner. He competed at schools level against other top prospects from across Great Britain, his record in these events improving as he became more experienced. Soon he was winning races, and this gave him confidence and belief in his ability. Mo continued his progress as a distance runner and in 2001 he competed in a 5,000-metre race against the best athletes in Europe. Mo won the title of European Junior Champion over the distance. At the age of 18, Mo had won his last event before becoming a full-time athlete.

Mo's career continued on an upward curve. He was now a very focused and disciplined athlete who trained hard. He did not have a social life, and there were no parties or other events to take his focus away from his career. His competiveness and single-mindedness were crucial aspects in his development as an athlete, and this commitment was starting to pay off with good results. In 2006, Mo took part in the **European Championships** in Gothenburg, Sweden, and finished second in the 5,000-metre race, gaining a silver medal for his achievement. This success was quickly followed by a win at the European Cross Country Championships in Italy.

Mo leads the rest of the pack in a cross-country race in 2001.

Mo celebrates with the race winner Jesus Espana after finishing as runner-up in the 5,000 metres at the 2006 European Championships.

Legend lends a hand

Paula Radcliffe, the world-famous long-distance runner and marathon world record holder, spotted Mo's potential as a world-class athlete from an early stage. She helped Mo by funding part of his training and also paid for him to learn to drive. Being able to drive meant that Mo did not have to rely on others to get around, and he gained some independence.

Mo's first experience of competing at the Olympics was an unhappy time for him. Despite all of the training and preparation for the 2008 Games in Beijing, he did not make it into the final of the 5,000-metre race. Mo described it as "the most disappointed I have ever been in my life." Mo responded by training even harder. He decided that he needed to train at higher **altitude** to really compete with the very best distance runners in the world.

Mo trained in Kenya and Ethiopia, in Africa, alongside world-class athletes, and when he returned to competition it was clear that the extra training had paid off. Of his time there, he has said, "Everything [there] is just focused, with nothing else. No distractions, no watching TV, no going to the cinema or any other things. Just focus. As an athlete, that's what you have to do."

European success

Mo began 2010 by setting a new British record over the 10,000-metre distance in a road race. He followed this result with more altitude training in Africa before returning to Europe for the European Championships.

Mo's performance at the competition in Barcelona was impressive. He won his first major athletics gold medal when he finished in first place in the 10,000 metres. His result also gave Great Britain its first gold medal at the championships that year. When Mo was asked about his success and the sacrifices he had made, he said, "It's hard work. I've spent so much time away from my family, it's not easy."

Mo followed up this success with another win in the 5,000 metres. In the closing stages of the gruelling race, Mo made it clear that he intended to win by surging through the field, crossing the finish line two seconds ahead of his closest challenger. In the immediate **aftermath** of the race Mo sank to his knees and offered a small prayer before he was congratulated by his opponents.

Mo pauses on the track after winning his first ever gold medal at a major athletics event.

Mo's first opportunity to test himself against the best distance runners in the world had come at the 2007 World Championships in Osaka, Japan. Mo finished in sixth position in the 5,000-metre race. Two years later, competing in the 5,000 metres again in Berlin, Germany, Mo finished in seventh place. He had proved that he clearly had the ability to run and compete at this level, but he had so far been unable to match the greatest runners. Mo needed to really push himself to improve that little bit more, and convince himself that he could win. His major breakthrough at the World Championships finally came in 2011.

Trying too hard? Mo trips during a race at the 2007 World Championships.

Mo celebrates on the track after winning the 5,000-metre race at the 2011 World Championships in South Korea.

Mo's third attempt to win a medal at the World Championships came in Daegu, South Korea. He showed how much he had improved and come to believe in himself. His performance was almost perfect. After finishing second in the 10,000 metres and winning his first ever World Championship medal, he went on to win the gold medal in the 5,000 metres. This was a magnificent performance and something that had never been achieved before by a British athlete.

THE WORLD CHAMPIONSHIPS

The World Championships take place every two years, and are held in a different country each time. Thousands of athletes represent their countries in a selection of track and field events at this major athletics event. For the athletes taking part, and millions of spectators, the popularity and prestige of the World Championships are second only to the Olympics Games.

In the early part of 2011, Mo had made the decision to change his coach. He stopped working with his long-time coach Alan Storey and began training with Alberto Salazar in the United States.

Moving to the United States

Mo and his family made the decision to move from Great Britain to Portland, Oregon, on the west coast of the United States. Mo's new coach was already living in the area and he persuaded Mo that his best chance of future success would be to live in Portland and train with him every day. By this time, Mo was married with a stepdaughter, so moving to another country was a big decision. Luckily it has proved to be the correct decision as Mo's results improved dramatically after the move, **culminating** in his triumphs at the Olympic Games in 2012.

After his move to Oregon, Mo began winning race after race.

Marathon legend Alberto Salazar crosses the finish line of the 1982 New York marathon to win the event for the third time in his career.

MO'S COACH

Alberto Salazar has been Mo's coach since 2011. Salazar is a legend in distance running, making him the ideal person to coach Mo in the lead up to the London 2012 Olympics. During his own impressive athletics career, Salazar won the New York marathon three years running (1980–1982), and he later went on to compete in ultra-marathons, races run over huge distances. In 2001, he set up "The Oregon Project" to help develop American long-distance athletes, and he invited Mo to join the project in 2010.

Saturday 4 August 2012 has become known in Great Britain as "Super Saturday". This was in response to the most successful day in the history of British track and field athletics. Mo played a huge part in this **momentous** day for British athletics, winning the home nation's third gold medal of the day when he finished in first position in the 10,000-metre race. Earlier that evening, Mo's teammates Jessica Ennis and Greg Rutherford had already achieved first place and gold medals in their events of the heptathlon and long jump. Within an hour of Jessica's win in the heptathlon, Britain's gold medal tally for the night was up to three following Mo's fabulous run.

Incredible atmosphere

The atmosphere created by the 80,000 **ecstatic** athletics fans in the stadium was incredible and it seemed that **Team GB** was feeding off their excitement. The crowd cheered wildly for the British athletes as they completed their events, and the noise seemed to build to a **crescendo** when Mo delivered his golden moment, crossing the finish line ahead of his competitors in the 10,000 metres.

Mo and Greg Rutherford celebrate together after creating Olympic history on "Super Saturday".

A delighted Mo holds up one of his Olympic gold medals.

THE OLYMPIC GAMES

The Olympic Games are the most famous athletics championships in the world. This **prestigious** event is held every four years in a different country. The most recent Olympic Games were held in London in 2012, with the next games taking place in Rio de Janeiro, Brazil, in 2016. The Olympic Games bring together more than 10,000 athletes from all over the world to compete in a total of 26 different sports. Winning a medal at the Olympics is a massive achievement, and winning a gold medal can change an athlete's life!

Mo followed up his incredible 10,000-metre Olympic title with the race of his life in the 5,000-metre race, seven days later. No British athlete had ever won the 10,000 metres at the Olympics before, so Mo had already created history. He continued to set new standards when he completed the long-distance double by winning the 5,000-metre race. The 5,000 metres was a tough race, with Mo competing against the best long-distance runners in the world for the second time in a week. He stuck to his plan to lead the race and, when the final lap began, increased his speed. He held off his competitors and he crossed the finish line with a huge smile on his face.

The Mobot

After Mo had crossed the finish line he also made a gesture with his hands. The gesture has become known as the Mobot, and the move is almost as famous as the man who performs it. Athletics fans all over Britain began to imitate the Mobot. Even legendary sprinter and London 2012 gold medallist Usain Bolt wanted to copy Mo. The two athletes were pictured together following Mo's successful run, with Usain doing the Mobot and Mo positioned in Usain's famous victory pose.

Doing the Mobot! Mo celebrates on track following his double Olympic gold medal success.

Superstar sprinter Usain Bolt joins in the celebrations with Mo and tries to copy the Mobot.

Impressive record

Mo is only the seventh athlete in history to win both the 5,000 and 10,000 metres at the Olympics. He joins a list of world-class athletes who have achieved the same.

5,000-METRE AND 10,000-METRE DOUBLE OLYMPIC CHAMPIONS	
1912	Hannes Kolehmainen (Finland)
1952	Emil Zátopek (Czechoslovakia)
1956	Vladimir Kuts (Russia)
1972 and 1976	Lasse Virén (Finland)
1980	Miruts Yifter (Ethiopia)
2008	Kenenisa Bekele (Ethiopia)
2012	Mo Farah (Great Britain)

In recent years, Mo's athletic performance has improved enormously, leading to him winning important races and collecting gold medals at major international athletics events. This success has made Mo a very recognizable figure in Great Britain and around the world, with his popularity increasing at the same time.

On top of his on-track success, Mo has received recognition by being named European Male Athlete of the Year in 2011 and 2012. His combination of talent and popularity make him exactly the type of person that companies approach to help them advertise their products. Mo already has lucrative contracts with major companies such as Nike and Lucozade. He could go on to earn millions of pounds from advertising contracts and **sponsorship**.

Charity work

Mo and his wife Tania visited his homeland of Somalia in 2011 and were shocked to see the devastation caused by a terrible drought. In response to this, Mo and Tania decided to set up the Mo Farah Foundation to raise money and awareness for the region.

Mo hopes that his foundation will provide long-term solutions to help people in East Africa gain access to clean water, **agricultural** supplies, and medical support. The foundation also supports existing community schools and establishes new schools in remote areas with the hope of providing poor children with a brighter future through education.

In 2012, the Foundation started up the "Do The Mobot" campaign, encouraging everyone to do a Mobot dance in order to raise £100,000 towards the Mo Farah Orphanage & Sports Academy.

Helping to raise funds

Mo and other British athletes, such as the 2008 Olympic 400-metre gold medallist Christine Ohuruogu, have donated photographs of themselves to Positive East, an **HIV** charity based in London. The money raised from an auction of the photographs will be used to help and support people with the disease.

Mo passes on his experience and advice to potential athletics stars of the future.

Mo appearing on British breakfast television show Daybreak *after his Olympic success.*

Since his outstanding performance at the London 2012 Olympic Games, Mo's popularity has rocketed. While some athletics fans knew who he was before the Games, now there are only a few people in Great Britain who wouldn't recognize his face! Mo has a great personality and he is often invited to appear on television chat shows and quiz programmes.

In a league of his own

In October 2012, Mo made an appearance on the popular television show *A League of Their Own*. The programme features a host and two team captains who are joined each week by popular sportspeople and comedians to take part in a quiz. Mo's popularity with viewers and his great sense of humour make him an ideal guest for a television sports quiz. It was during one of Mo's earlier appearances on the show that the now famous Mobot pose was invented. The sports presenter Clare Balding and the host James Corden came up with the idea of the pose and named it the Mobot!

Another set of twins

Mo's wife, Tania, gave birth to twins shortly after his outstanding performance at the London Olympics. Images of Mo celebrating after the races with his wife and stepdaughter Rhianna clearly showed that Tania was due to give birth very soon. The twin baby girls, Aisha and Amani, were born on 24 August, just 13 days after Mo's success in the 5,000-metre race. Being a twin himself, Mo may have suspected that he would have twins one day, as this is something that often passes from one generation to the next.

Mo is joined by Tania and Rhianna to celebrate on the track following his incredible win in the London 2012 10,000-metre race.

Mo's coach, Alberto Salazar, was interviewed by BBC radio in October 2012. An important question related to the possible events Mo could compete in at the 2016 Olympic Games in Rio de Janeiro, Brazil. Salazar revealed it is most likely that Mo will go for a double again, but instead of 5,000 metres and 10,000 metres, he might compete in the 10,000 metres and the marathon. Salazar said, "My guess is that he will do a 10-marathon double. At Rio that would be a good shot. We will have to look at the schedule." Mo's chances will depend on whether there is enough time between the events to recover, but if the scheduling works in his favour, he will attempt the 10,000 metres and the marathon at the same Olympics. This has been attempted before by a handful of great athletes, but you have to go all the way back to the 1952 Olympics, and legend Emil Zátopek, to find an athlete who actually accomplished the feat. If Mo succeeds in both races in 2016 it would be an incredible achievement.

Bright future

Mo always seems to have a smile on his face. He appears to handle the pressure that comes with being a top athlete and national hero without any trouble, and he seems perfectly comfortable being one of the most recognizable faces in Britain. Whatever Mo decides to do in the future, he is likely to do very well. He has been so successful on and off the track in recent years that he, and his many fans, can look forward to many more incredible performances.

Czech Emil Zátopek was the last athlete to win gold medals at both the 10,000 metres and the marathon, at the 1952 Olympic Games. He also won the 5,000 metres.

Mo and the US athlete Galen Rupp prepare together for another gruelling distance race.

TIMELINE

1983   Mohamed Farah is born in Mogadishu, Somalia.

1991   Mo moves to London, England.

2001   Mo wins the 5,000-metre European Junior title.

2006   Mo wins a silver medal at the European Championships.

            Mo wins the European Cross Country Championships in San Giorgio, Italy.

2007   Mo competes in the 5,000 metres at the World Championships in Osaka, Japan, finishing sixth.

2008   Mo fails to qualify for the final of the 5,000 metres at the Beijing Olympics.

2009   Mo competes in the 5,000 metres at the World Championships in Berlin, Germany, finishing seventh.

2010   Mo wins the 5,000 and 10,000 metres at the European Championships in Barcelona, Spain.

2011   Mo moves to the United States to train with Alberto Salazar in Portland, Oregon.

            Mo becomes the first British male athlete in history to win the World Championships 5,000-metre title. He also wins a silver medal in the 10,000 metres.

            Mo wins the title of European Male Athlete of the Year.

2012   Mo wins the men's 5,000 metres at the 2012 European Athletics Championships, held in Helsinki, Finland.

            Mo wins the 5,000 and 10,000 metres at the London 2012 Olympics.

            Mo is awarded the title of European Male Athlete of the Year again.

Mo's loves football and can be seen regularly supporting his beloved Arsenal at their stadium, the Emirates.

 Mo and his wife Tania met when they were both still at school.

 Mo is a practising **Muslim** and usually prays before a race.

 Two postboxes in London were painted gold by the Royal Mail to celebrate Mo's success at the London 2012 Olympics.

 Mo uses a special underwater treadmill when he is training. By using this special piece of training equipment, and not running outdoors, Mo can reduce the risk of injury.

 In 2012, Mo took part in a popular television game show *The Cube* and won £250,000 for charity. He donated the money to the Mo Farah Foundation.

Mo's golden postboxes can be found in the Greater London areas of Isleworth and Teddington.

GLOSSARY

aftermath something that results or follows from an event

agricultural to do with farming

altitude height of something, especially above sea-level

civil war war fought between people living in the same country

coach person who helps an athlete to train and win competitions

crescendo gradual, steady increase in loudness or force

culminating reaching the highest point

ecstatic feeling great delight or joy

European Championships athletics event held every two years. Only athletes from European countries can take part in these championships.

HIV Human immunodeficiency virus. A virus that attacks the body's immune system.

momentous very important

Muslim person who follows the religion of Islam

prestigious something that is respected because it is important or of a high quality

role model person who is looked up to by others as an example

sacrifice give up something so that another good thing may happen

sponsorship when money is provided by one person or organization to support another person

Team GB name given to the British team at the London 2012 Olympic Games

Books

Mo Farah, Roy Apps (Franklin Watts, 2012)

Olympic Champions, Nick Hunter (Wayland, 2011)

Olympic Stars, Laura Durman (Franklin Watts, 2011)

The London Olympics 2012, Nick Hunter (Raintree, 2011)

Websites

Aviva Startrack
http://academy.uka.org.uk/startrack/
If you would like to take up athletics, visit this website to find out about sessions near you.

UK Athletics
http://www.uka.org.uk
Visit the UK Athletics website to find out about future athletics events and get news about British athletes.

London 2012
http://www.london2012.com
Find out more about the London 2012 Olympic Games on this website.

INDEX